[ir]Relevant Youth Ministry
Making it Matter

Study Guide for
Parents and Volunteers

Randy DonGiovanni
with Greg Smith

Copyright © 2012 by Randy DonGiovanni
This is a work of nonfiction. Any resemblance to actual persons, organizations, or events are purely coincidence.

All rights reserved by the author, including the right of reproduction in whole or in part in any form.

Cover design by Greg Smith of Black Lake Studio.

Published by Black Lake Press of Holland, Michigan.
Black Lake Press is a division of Black Lake Studio, LLC.
Direct inquiries to Black Lake Press at
www.blacklakepress.com.

ISBN 978-1480162471

Scriptures taken from the Holy Bible,
New International Version ®, NIV®.
Copyright © 1973, 1978, 1984, 2011 by Biblica, Inc.™
Used by permission of Zondervan.
All rights reserved worldwide.
www.zondervan.com

Table of Contents

	How to Use This Workbook	9
	Introduction: Let's Make it Matter	11
1	The Gospel is Good Enough	17
2	Randy's Story	21
3	It's Not About Us	25
4	Destiny Determines Identity	31
5	Follow Jesus, Not Pop Culture and Trends	35
6	The Seduction of Short-Term Missions	39
7	Who Has the Youth Pastor's Back?	43
8	Why Youth Pastors and Senior Staff Need Each Other	47
9	It Takes a Village: Why the Congregation Needs to Get Involved	53
10	There Are People Doing it Right	57
11	Fathers and Mothers	61

12	Undermining the Gospel at Home	65
13	Jesus Freaks	69
14	Why it's Worth It	73
15	Is There Hope for Youth Ministry in America?	77
	Conclusion: It's Time to be [ir]Relevant	81

How to Use This Workbook

This study guide is designed to be a companion to Randy DonGiovanni's book, *[ir]Relevant Youth Ministry: Making it Matter*. This guide can be used for personal study; however, it is recommended that this book be used in a small-group setting to ensure participation and encouragement through discussion (i.e. adult Sunday School class, small group, home church, etc.). It is also recommended that this book be used in a sixteen-to-eighteen-week study–one chapter per week.

Introduction: Let's Make it Matter

Matthew 28:19-20: "Therefore go and make disciples of all nations, baptizing them in the name of the Father and of the Son and of the Holy Spirit, and teaching them to obey everything I have commanded you." The Great Commission calls each and every one of us into ministry. As we bring the Gospel of Jesus Christ to those in need, let us not forget the youth at our own back doors–in our homes, in our neighborhoods, in our churches, and in our schools. Youth today have the same need as the youth of the past (we all need Jesus), but times are changing and so are the methods of delivering the Gospel. Youth ministry isn't working the same way it was 10, 15, 20, even 30 years ago. We are losing kids, we are losing heart, and we are burning out. So what are we doing wrong? A huge part of the problem is that we are trying too hard to be relevant to pop-culture and forgetting or foregoing being relevant to the Gospel.

Discussion Questions

Discuss the three goals of youth ministry:

1. Lead the teens in our care to accept Christ as their savior.

_____

_____

_____

_____

_____

2. Teach them to obey His commands and live as one of His followers.

_____

_____

_____

_____

_____

3. Grow up to become part of and actively participate in His body, the Church.

_____
_____
_____
_____
_____

Read through the following statistics about today's churched youth again:

- 63% don't believe Jesus is the Son of the one true God.
- 58% believe all faiths teach equally valid truths.
- 51% don't believe Jesus rose from the dead.
- 65% don't believe Satan is a real entity.
- 68% don't believe the Holy Spirit is a real entity.
- 64% believe if a person is generally good or does enough good things for others they will earn a place in heaven.
- 81% believe all truth relates to the individual.
- 72% say it's true if it works for you.
- 85% of evangelical youth "drop out" of church between 10th-12th grade.

Are these statistics what you'd expect? Are they shocking? What did you think would have been different?

_____
_____
_____
_____
_____

Why has the American Church been steadily losing its kids over the last ten to twenty years?

_____
_____
_____
_____
_____
_____

Where are we going in youth ministry?

_____
_____
_____

_____

_____

How do you think youth ministry will look different in twenty years?

_____

_____

_____

_____

What role will you play in helping youth ministry become more successful?

_____

_____

_____

_____

_____

Notes:

_____

_____

Chapter 1
The Gospel is Good Enough

In chapter one, I describe the hiring process of a youth pastor in my friend's church. After years of stagnation, this church was looking to revitalize its youth ministry. The church implemented what they thought was the perfect ministry plan and began the hiring process of a new youth pastor. This plan and pastor would be responsible for bringing new vision to the program and ultimately bringing more youth into the church. The church received numerous applicants for the position, but they couldn't find the right fit. As a fifty-year-old uneducated handyman, Jim wasn't the ideal candidate the elders envisioned for their church, but after a prompting by the Holy Spirit, the senior pastor called Jim in for an interview. Jim didn't have an elaborate plan for ministry, but he instead had a profound belief in the word of God.

He knew that the Bible could stand on its own as the greatest book of instructions and plans. This is what made Jim remarkable. My friend's story reminds me of the apostle Paul. "Paul wasn't cool. He wasn't successful in ministry because he was charismatic." What Paul did, and what Jim did, was to proclaim the Gospel of Jesus Christ with complete conviction and integrity. Does your church's ministry do the same?

Discussion Questions

In your ministry (whatever ministry you do), are you brave enough to let the Gospel stand on its own?

_____

_____

_____

_____

_____

What are some things that are standing in the way?

_____

_____

[ir]Relevant Youth Ministry

_____
_____
_____

We are sometimes so focused on the "plan" that we forget to take time to listen to God and figure out what He really wants for us and our ministries. Isn't the Gospel good enough? Do you ever find yourself too focused on the "plan?" Describe a time when you did. How can you or did you remember that the Word of God can indeed stand on its own?

_____
_____
_____
_____
_____
_____
_____

Notes:

_____
_____

Randy DonGiovanni

_____
_____
_____

Chapter 2
Randy's Story

"Jesus got my attention when I was eight years old," when I heard coach Tom Landry of the Dallas Cowboys give his testimony on the television. I was raised in my grandparents home, and I saw the tangible love of Jesus there. Both of my grandparents played a pivotal role in my development not only as a young man but also as a follower of Christ. They are the ones who planted the seed of youth ministry in my heart. It wasn't until my late high-school years that I really began to listen to the calling that my Father had placed on my life, but when I did, I knew my life would never look the same again. This was the beginning of the twenty-eight years that I've spent in youth ministry, and God willing, I have decades more to give. Over these years, I have watched the culture of youth change, but God doesn't change, nor have the hearts of our kids. This is what I was called to do, and this is where I belong.

Discussion Questions:

Was there any part of Randy's story that you connected with personally? Why?

_____
_____
_____
_____
_____

Reflect on the desires, wants, needs, or hurts you experienced as an adolescent. Do you think adolescents of today experience these same feelings? Why or why not?

_____
_____
_____
_____
_____

[ir]Relevant Youth Ministry

Is there someone in your life who has nurtured you and has spoken truth into your life? Who planted an "evangelistic seed" in you? Take time to thank them and pray for them.

_____
_____
_____
_____
_____

Think of the people in your life. Whose soil is ready for seed? Whose life can you speak into?

_____
_____
_____
_____
_____

Notes:

_____
_____

Randy DonGiovanni

Chapter 3
It's Not About Us

"None of us sets out to be an egomaniac." I believe this is true for all of us, as followers of Jesus Christ, in whatever capacity we serve in ministry. We want to put forth our best effort; therefore, we only want and expect the best outcome. But somewhere between efforts and expectations, we somehow start to care more about ourselves than the work that we are doing for God's Kingdom. If our hearts are in the wrong place, then we lose our way. God as our Father, only wants the best for us: He wants us to be successful and effective, but He will not be pleased with what we are doing if we make it all about ourselves. When we talk about youth ministry in this context, as I've said in chapter three, the ministry becomes a business, and the kids become the customers. Do you see this happening in your church's youth ministry or in your own ministry (whatever it is that you give your time to)? Have you lost your joy? How can we remedy this mindset and prevent it from happening again?

Discussion Questions:

Let's take a closer look at a few of the ways we make our ministries about us:

We want to be liked, even loved. Who doesn't want to be liked? Someone who doesn't care about the affection and admiration of those he leads probably has too hard of a heart to be a great leader. But being liked has its limits. We should never put it ahead of doing the right thing, even if it won't make us popular with the kids or their parents or the congregation.

Do you worry about what others think of you? In what ways?

_____
_____
_____
_____

Have you ever compromised what's right in the eyes of the Father for the sake of popularity?

_____
_____
_____
_____

Are you trying to please people, or are you trying to please God?

_____
_____
_____
_____

We design the program around our desires. It can be tempting to build a ministry that's fun for us to lead. In youth ministry, if the students are a mostly captive audience (because their parents make them attend), a leader/pastor can find themselves picking activities and planning trips that appeal to themselves. A youth pastor/leader with a short attention span might build a ministry that is full of activity but short on consistent relationships.

I agree that any pastor/leader ought to lead with his spiritual gifts and personality and customize a program to fit his identity. But you should never bend your (youth) ministry into your dream job just because you can. If you're doing this, then it really is about you.

Take an honest look at yourself and whatever ministry you are doing. Are you making it about you? How much of your ministry is really planned for you?

_____

_____

_____

_____

_____

_____

We use youth ministry as a stepping stone. It's true; some youth pastors/leaders don't really want to be doing youth ministry. They want to pastor adults or become senior pastors or some other position higher up the church staff food chain. These kind of youth pastors/leaders see their job as an entry-level position. They figure that if they put a couple of years into it, they can get a promotion or at least use the youth ministry on their resume. They are auditioning for bigger and better things. Their heart is not really invested with the teens in the group, so they will never really invest for the long term with that group of teens.

Youth ministry is a calling all its own, a life-long calling. How can you be supportive to that calling in the pastors around you? How can you make them feel valued and appreciated? How can you let them know that you are on their side and support one of the greatest callings—to teach children and youth about the God who loves them unconditionally?

_____
_____
_____
_____
_____
_____
_____
_____

Randy DonGiovanni

Notes:

Chapter 4
Destiny Determines Identity

1 Peter 2:9-10 tells us that we are a chosen people and have been called out of darkness, and that we have received His mercy. God has a plan for each of us; He has a plan for our futures apart from our pasts. In chapter four, I explain my belief that we, a people who are created in the image of God, are not defined by our pasts but by our future identity in Christ. One of my favorite stories in my career as a youth pastor is about young lady named Mikayla. As she shared with me the stories of her difficult past, she told me how she felt unlovable. How could God love someone like her? Over time, I helped her to see herself through different eyes–through the perfect eyes of her heavenly Father. She was indeed loved, she was important, and her life had worth. Those of us in youth ministry are charged with showing these youth that they

are not the product of their pasts and that they have an opportunity to be reborn into Christ Jesus. We all need to be reminded of this as we walk alongside our brothers and sisters. They are worth it. Kids are worth it. And we should never give up.

Discussion Questions:

How can you see beyond someone's past like Jesus does? Are you able to see hope in their future?

_____

_____

_____

_____

_____

Think for a second about your own past and where you are now. Does seeing that the Lord was capable of turning you around give you hope for others?

_____

_____

[ir]Relevant Youth Ministry

_____
_____

How does understanding your identity in Jesus Christ shape or change your destiny?

_____
_____
_____
_____
_____

What do you think God's role for you in the Kingdom is?

_____
_____
_____
_____
_____

Notes:

_____
_____

Randy DonGiovanni

Chapter 5

Follow Jesus, Not Pop Culture and Trends

"Ignatius, the Ultimate Youth Pastor"—is your church's youth pastor like this guy? I sincerely hope not. While this video is of course a parody, it brings to light a very real problem that we have in today's youth ministry in churches across America. Because we see a continuous shift in culture, we strive to be relevant to it by keeping up on all the latest trends. This in itself isn't the problem. It's OK to be cool, hip, and trendy. But the problem comes in when we are trying too hard to be something we are not. If you or your youth pastor/leader feels comfortable donning that graphic tee and skinny jeans, by all means, do it. But if you'd rather be wearing loafers and a polo, then just stick with that. While we joke about this, this problem really runs deeper than fashion. It's serious. Kids are brilliant, and they see right through us. They don't want us to be fake, and they'll sniff us out in a heartbeat if we are. I've said it before, but I don't think it could be said enough: although culture changes, God doesn't. And the hearts of kids don't change either. Kids need a person they can trust in their lives, a person with genuine integrity. We need to make the Gospel matter to them, and show them how relevant Christ can be to their lives.

Discussion Questions:

What does it mean to be culturally relevant to a generation that is constantly changing and being defined by popular culture?

_____
_____
_____
_____
_____

How would you define pop culture?

_____
_____

_____
_____
_____

What do you think are some "bad" culture trends that are influencing kids today?

_____
_____
_____
_____
_____

Has your church fallen into the trap of chasing trends in its ministries church-wide?

_____
_____
_____
_____
_____

How can you make Christ relevant to the upcoming generation?

Randy DonGiovanni

Notes:

Chapter 6
The Seduction of Short-Term Missions

As well-meaning adults, we spend thousands of dollars flying our kids to different countries to see how people are living differently than us here in the United States. We send them on these short-term mission trips because we believe they are making a difference in the lives of those they serve. We want our kids to learn to evangelize to the nations. This is a noble goal, but in reality, the difference is made not in the lives of others but in the lives of the kids themselves. This is not to say that short-term missions aren't valuable—they are. On these types of trips, as kids see, help, and minister to people different from themselves, they become discipled and educated. Also, community and camaraderie are built within the youth ministry—all very important values in a thriving and spiritually filling ministry. But if we truly want to teach our kids to evangelize, we must not forget that there is a wide-open mission field right outside our church door.

Discussion Questions:

Do you think it's possible that encouraging short-term mission trips encourages a lifestyle of chasing the Jesus high instead of a steady and committed faith? Why or why not?

_____
_____
_____
_____
_____

How well does your church reach out to local people in need? How do they do this? Has your church ever considered doing a local mission trip?

_____
_____
_____

[ir]Relevant Youth Ministry

_____

_____

_____

Are short-term mission trips "worth it?" What are the ultimate goals of a short-term mission trip? How does this type of mission work align with or stray from how Jesus did ministry?

_____

_____

_____

_____

_____

_____

_____

Notes:

_____

_____

_____

_____

Chapter 7

Who Has the Youth Pastor's Back?

Is your church supportive of its pastors/leaders? Is there an encouraging and nurturing culture among your church's leaders? In chapter seven, I explain the necessity of needing each other. I tell the story of my friend, Tom, who was hired as a youth pastor in a church that boasted an "open door policy." Instead, Tom experienced quite the opposite. He was shut out, criticized, and dismissed without any help or care from his supervisors, particularly the senior pastor. It goes without saying that most pastors don't have a secret motive, hoping that the youth pastor fails. But in reality, it does unfortunately happen because, let's face it, everyone is busy doing their own things. We need to be mindful of this. Ultimately, it is the kids who suffer when there is an ever-revolving door of youth pastors who get burnt out due to lack of support. It it my heart that every person in ministry have someone that they can fall back on, someone who mentors them, encourages them, and has their back.

Discussion Questions:

As I asked in my book, if the senior pastor can't or won't work to initiate a nurturing culture, who will? Are you supportive of your youth pastor/leader?

_____
_____
_____
_____
_____

How can you show more support, and how can you encourage others to do the same? Perhaps you are the senior pastor; how can you be an encouragement to your youth pastor/leader?

_____
_____
_____

_____

_____

_____

_____

Does your church have a nurturing culture, allowing a young pastor or leader to grow, learn, and make mistakes along the way? Why or why not?

_____

_____

_____

_____

_____

Notes:

_____

_____

_____

_____

Chapter 8

Why Youth Pastors and Senior Staff Need Each Other

In chapter eight, we get a glimpse of the interactions between senior pastors and youth leaders. As politics and insecurity creep into the church's cracks through miscommunication, we come to understand why it is important that these two parties function cooperatively and communicate effectively. Our illustrations come from poorly established relationships between pastors and leaders. In all three anecdotes in this chapter, a senior pastor effectively shuts down a youth pastor/leader who, in some way or another, steals the congregational spotlight. As a congregation, we should submit to our leadership. At the same time, it's important to know what's going on in our church's leadership so that we know what to pray for them and what services we can offer. If you are an active member of your church congregation, I'm sure you are no stranger to politics. In fact, it's likely that you've seen it operate on some level that may have divided your church on an issue. As sad as it is, there have been many churches that have separated or disbanded over something as silly as an insecurity within the leadership. We have to continually refine ourselves, being prepared to rebuke out of a loving spirit and forgive with the grace that comes from Christ.

Discussion Questions:

What steps do we need to develop healthy relationships with our church leadership?

_____

_____

_____

_____

_____

How, as parents and volunteers, can we grow in a spirit of submission to the senior pastor?

[ir]Relevant Youth Ministry

_____
_____
_____
_____
_____

Have you ever witnessed the friction between two pastors dividing your church? What was your reaction? If you have not, how would you ideally hope to react?

_____
_____
_____
_____
_____
_____
_____
_____

What can you as a congregation member do in that situation?

Randy DonGiovanni

_____
_____
_____
_____
_____

How hard or easy is it to forgive our pastors when we feel that they have misled us in some way?

_____
_____
_____
_____
_____
_____

Where does the grace to forgive come from?

_____
_____
_____
_____
_____

[ir]Relevant Youth Ministry

Notes:

Chapter 9

It Takes a Village: Why the Congregation Needs to Get Involved

In chapter nine, we hear the story of a self-sacrificing congregation. Their humility is admirable, and in an effort to reach the lost teens, some ministries gave up their funds, risked the danger of gangs and violence on their grounds, and prayed fervently. The first Church in the book of Acts does something very similar. They offer up their commodities for the greater good of the growing Church. Unity within the Church body is beautiful, yet we don't often see it. However, when we do catch a glimpse of it, such as in the anecdote about Matt rallying the congregation to help reach lost teenagers, it strengthens our faith. We see what a united Church body is capable of, and the testimony motivates us to set aside our differences as a congregation, seek the Lord together, and obey the direction in which He leads our greater body.

Discussion Questions:

Take a look at your own congregation. In terms of programs, ministries, budget, and goals, is the body unified? In what ways is your church moving toward Christ together, and in what ways do you feel church forces opposing one another?

_____
_____
_____
_____
_____
_____
_____

In order for Matt's church to reach the lost, they had to be willing to sacrifice in other areas of their congregation. Think about the areas of the church you are involved in. If an opportunity arose to reach people outside of your area, how willing would you be to let go of funds and possibly security in order to make it work?

[ir]Relevant Youth Ministry

Is it difficult to invest in an area that you don't get to be a part of or see the fruit of? Why or why not?

In what ministries is your church most unified? Divided?

Randy DonGiovanni

Notes:

Chapter 10
There Are People Doing it Right

Chapter ten gives us anecdotes about successful youth ministers. One of them, Eran Holt, plugged his students into different ministries based on their passions. As older members of the congregation, it can be tempting to see a teenager's offer to help as nice but ineffective. If we're honest with ourselves, sometimes we question whether young and rowdy teens can be anything more than a distraction.

What we have to remember is that these kids have the same Holy Spirit we do. Wisdom comes with age, but it comes faster with God. Is it possible we could learn something from teenagers? Imagine a church where instead of middle schoolers running up and down the halls and making noise, growing teenagers worked alongside children and senior citizen ministries, being discipled by adults entrusted with those ministries and using all that energy towards building Christ's body. Is it possible that our frustrations with kids this age come from our own inability to disciple them, love them where they're at, and serve alongside them?

Discussion Questions:

How, as a congregation, can we actively invite teenagers to partner with us in the ministries we oversee?

_____

_____

_____

_____

_____

Is it tempting to label teenagers as ineffective or as distractions?

_____

_____

_____

[ir]Relevant Youth Ministry

_____

_____

Have you ever been humbled by seeing a young person chasing or serving Christ in such a passionate way that it made you reexamine your own faith? If not, are you doing anything to empower the youth to become such young men and women of the Lord?

_____

_____

_____

_____

_____

Notes:

_____

_____

_____

_____

Chapter 11
Fathers and Mothers

In chapter eleven, we understand how mothers and fathers play a large role in shaping their children's faith. As members of the church congregation, many of you probably have children. Since much of the church body in America today is made up of familial units, this may be a good time for self-reflection. Take an honest look at your parental role and ask, how am I doing when my only standard is reflecting Christ to my children? Ignore the PTO meetings, forget about whether or not you gave your kid the best education, and focus solely on how you mirror Christ. Is this happening? For those of you who don't have children, God still calls you to live in community with his body, and that includes the youth. While you may not be called to be a mother or father in a young person's life, God may use you to be a mentor–someone who listens to the youth, challenges their thinking on things, loves them where they are at, and walks alongside of them as they grow and mature in their faith. This is a noble pursuit, and while many teens probably will not say it, they are hungry for the wisdom of older people and will usually flock to the oldest person who takes them seriously.

Discussion Questions:

For those of you who are parents, how are you doing at reflecting Christ to your children?

_____
_____
_____
_____
_____

In Scripture, God calls his people over and over again to look after the widows and the orphans. I'm sure we don't have to look far to see youth in our congregation whose parents are either divorced or absent. How can we be mothers and fathers–or mentors–to these kids?

[ir]Relevant Youth Ministry

_____
_____
_____
_____
_____

Have you ever considered being a mentor to a young person who is not your child or relative? How might this impact his or her faith journey?

_____
_____
_____
_____
_____

Notes:

_____
_____
_____
_____
_____

Chapter 12
Undermining the Gospel at Home

Again, many of us are parents. The temptation is to read over the stories of "terrible" parents in this chapter and breathe a sigh of relief as we realize that none of us would ever undermine the Gospel in such a way in our own homes. Maybe you've grown up in the church your whole life. Maybe you've raised your kids in the same faith tradition you had, doing everything you could to point them to Christ. But if we really want to be Christ-like, we have to recognize that areas exist where we fall short. God is the only perfect parent. For no other purpose than our own personal growth and a desire to be refined, it's important to ask ourselves what areas of our parenthood aren't honoring to Christ. It could be something as simple as how we spend our time and money. It's also important to recognize, as stated in the chapter, that youth pastors/

leaders are there to walk alongside kids, not take over as their parents. It's human nature to feel jealous of someone who seems to be connecting to our kids better than we do, but we have to keep a proper perspective in mind.

Discussion Questions:

Think of a time you have been frustrated by your own children or other young people. What was your initial reaction? Did this exemplify or point away from Christ's humility?

_____
_____
_____
_____
_____

What are some ways in which God has empowered you to be a great parent? In which areas do you fall short?

_____
_____
_____

[ir]Relevant Youth Ministry

Do you ever feel threatened by a youth pastor/leader who seems to be taking over your role in your children's lives?

Notes:

Chapter 13
Jesus Freaks

Passionless love. It's one of the things that stands out most in this chapter. In no way do I think this is true for everyone, but as a general trend, people tend to lose passion with age. Yet Jesus said that he wouldn't settle for passionless love (see Revelation 3:15). How do we as a congregation renew our passion and energy for the Gospel? We look to the youth. Young people possess a passion and energy that we lose with time. That's why it's so important for the church body to be diversified by age: we need each other. As older members of the congregation, we need the encouragement found in watching young people get a hold of the Spirit's fire. And young people need the wisdom of their elders, lest their passion be misguided by every wind of false teaching. We can't afford to stomp out the passion of the youth by shooting down their ideas or neglecting to worry about their discipleship. They are an asset to our congregations, and the church will not thrive unless we all choose to sharpen one another.

Discussion Questions:

Is "passionate" a word you would use to describe your walk with the Lord? Why or why not?

_____

_____

_____

_____

_____

Can you think of any wise people that poured into you when you were younger? How did their counsel shape the course of your faith? What are some ways that we can now share that wisdom with younger people in the congregation?

_____

_____

_____

[ir]Relevant Youth Ministry

_____
_____
_____
_____
_____
_____
_____

Can you think of a time where a younger person's passion for the Gospel affected you? What was that like?

_____
_____
_____
_____
_____

Notes:

_____
_____
_____
_____
_____

Chapter 14
Why it's Worth It

In chapter fourteen, I confess my own struggles in youth ministry. It's tiring, and though I hate to admit it, I'm getting older. Within your congregation, someone is in charge of heading up the youth ministry. They may be older like me or younger, but either way, their job is—while rewarding—probably tiring. Youth pastors are also some of the most criticized people in the church. In my own experience, I've seen parents constantly putting youth pastors under the microscope and examining their every action. While this can be healthy, when it isn't done out of a spirit of love and refinement, it becomes a source of anxiety for the youth minister. By hiring on the youth pastor, we've acknowledged as a congregation that he or she is capable for the job and a good fit. The least we can do once they are in the position is encourage them. We've entrusted them with our youth. Why not build them up with the love of Christ instead of criticism? Then, they can pass on that love to the youth.

Discussion Questions:

What are some ways you can love on youth pastors and encourage them?

_____
_____
_____
_____
_____

Why is this important?

_____
_____
_____

What are some struggles that a youth minister might encounter within your specific congregation? How can you help them through these struggles?

[ir]Relevant Youth Ministry

How does one examine the work of a pastor/leader with a spirit of love and refinement instead of judgment and fault-finding?

Notes:

Chapter 15
Is There Hope for Youth Ministry in America?

Is there hope for youth ministry in America? Sometimes, it's hard to see it with all the political battles in the church, the difficulty with parent relationships, the constant spiritual warfare, and the new lows that pop culture is taking kids to. Yet, despite all of this, Christ's finished work on the cross is stronger. He tells us to take heart because He has overcome the world (see John 16:33) and that all authority on heaven and earth has been given to Him (Matthew 28:18). The chapter also warns us against becoming like the Laodecians, who had monetary wealth but were in spiritual poverty. As a congregation member who is perhaps not directly involved in youth ministry, you still have a role to play. You can act as a source of accountability and raise the question of whether or not your church's youth ministry is pursuing Christ or pursuing culture. While it's important to remember that all rebuke should come from love, I don't think it's a bad thing to ask your youth pastor/leader–in a friendly way– what they are doing to ensure that Christ is being preached over culture. Youth pastors/leaders may even grow from that experience.

Discussion Questions:

Is there hope for the future of youth ministry within your church?

_____

_____

_____

_____

What makes it look promising? What makes it look bleak?

_____

_____

_____

[[ir]Relevant Youth Ministry

_____

_____

Though it's scary, take a moment and compare your youth ministry to the church of Laodecia. Does your church have all the technology and toys but still feel like it is lacking something?

_____

_____

_____

_____

_____

Are you directly involved in your youth ministry? If not, do you have an interest in how it is going?

_____

_____

_____

_____

_____

Randy DonGiovanni

Have you ever had a conversation about Christ versus culture in the context of youth ministry within your congregation?

Notes:

Conclusion: It's Time to be [ir]Relevant

The conclusion is a time for reflection–to assess our youth ministries and ask whether they are conforming to culture to try to win kids to Jesus or presenting the truth of the Gospel without regard to culture. In the chapter, I also point out that in today's society, fathers are often portrayed on television as abusive, clueless, or as buffoons. Considering that we are sons and daughters of the Heavenly Father, I believe that we, as his church, have a responsibility to reconcile the image of a father to this upcoming generation–especially since a number of us in the congregation are fathers.

"Dear friends, I urge you, as foreigners and exiles, to abstain from sinful desires, which wage war against your soul. Live such good lives among the pagans that, though they accuse you of doing wrong, they may see your good deeds and glorify God on the day he visits us" (1 Peter 2:11-12).

Discussion Questions:

Overall, how is your church's youth ministry doing?

_____

_____

_____

_____

_____

Do you feel that it is trying to appeal to culture or presenting the Gospel without trying to dress it up to match the latest television fashion?

_____

_____

_____

_____

_____

[ir]Relevant Youth Ministry

How can we reconcile the image of fathers in the upcoming generation?

What role does the church play in that?

How can we reflect the Heavenly Father?

Randy DonGiovanni

Notes:

About the Author

Randy DonGiovanni is a graduate of Valley Forge Christian College in Phoenixville, PA. He also attended West Chester University in West Chester, PA.

Randy and his wife Lori have worked with youth and young adults for over twenty-seven years. In addition, Randy was the former Speed-the-Light and Youth Alive Director in the state of Michigan.

He has experience in speaking to students at rallies, retreats, camps, high schools, and college campuses all over the nation.

Randy has a sincere desire and vision is to be used by the Lord in seeing lives radically changed for the kingdom of God. Through practical application of scripture, humor, and story-telling, Randy motivates and encourages young people to live a committed and Spirit-filled life.

For more information about RandyDon Ministries, please visit Randy's website at randydon.org.